FINANCIAL GOALS

A handbook on personal finance for young working adults

SK Read

ISBN: 978-981-14-7013-4

"A terrific book…a gift to every reader who picks it up…seasoned with lived wisdom"
— Michelle Martin, *Your Money on Money FM 89.3, SPH Radio*

"*Financial Goals* is an invaluable gift of wisdom and practical knowledge on personal finance. A good read that is simple to understand, yet practical."
— Chia Pee Teck, Financial Consultant, *Prudential Assurance Co. Singapore*

"Very easy to read and backed up with good evidence. I will definitely implement some of his ideas."
— Dr. Vivek Goodoory, Medical Doctor, *Leeds Teaching Hospitals NHS Trust, UK*

"In this period of easy credit and an abundance of things to spend money on, it provides good sage advice."
— Mithran Doraisamy, Senior Partner, *Korn Ferry, Australia*

"I'm going to get a bunch of this book for my nephews and nieces who are just starting out in their careers; come to think of it, maybe for a few of my adult friends as well!"
— Oliver Foo, Managing Partner, *Edge Consulting LLP, Singapore*

For

My wonderful sons as their life journeys
continue

Contents

Preface

I was the managing director of a joint venture manufacturing company where I worked for twenty-six years. When our company ceased operations, my personal financial situation was less than ideal. This book is not about the circumstances that led to my predicament, but those very same circumstances certainly motivated me to write it. I was determined that my children recognize, early on in their lives, the need for financial security. It was written following a talk my wife and I had with our two young adult sons who were just starting their careers. The focus of our discussion was on what should be one of their main goals in life, namely financial security, and how to chart a path towards achieving that goal. While attaining financial independence is an ideal, my emphasis was on homeownership and building up adequate retirement savings.

Realizing how overwhelmed my sons were by the volume and seriousness of the information I shared, I decided to pen it all down in this handbook. I call it a handbook because different chapters are likely to prove relevant at different points in their careers; they can always revisit one or more chapters in an effort to stay on the right track towards meeting their financial goals. Furthermore, having a glimpse of what possibly lies ahead in the later chapters of one's life gives a person a sense of direction and motivation to push on with one's endeavours.

Finally, I decided to write this book because the essence of the message I communicated to my sons is a common concern which all parents share and which young adults eventually realize. The goal of financial security is inherent in all of us regardless of our socioeconomic position in life. We are all, knowingly or not, on the same journey towards the same financial goal.

Chapter 1

Orbit of Familiarity versus Orbit of Similarity

I have always encouraged my sons to think objectively before forming an opinion on an issue, reacting to a situation or thinking of possible solutions to a problem. Similarly I feel that any kind of advice rendered is more likely to be taken into consideration if it is based on objective analysis followed by logical discussion.

I started the talk with my young adult sons by providing context to my advice on financial planning. It was important to begin by emphasizing the distinction between one's *orbit of familiarity* and one's *orbit of similarity*.

We are familiar with relationships extending from the immediate family to grandparents, aunts and uncles, cousins, friends, distant relatives and other acquaintances in our community. It is natural to assume that most of the people in our orbit, being in the same social community, share a similar socioeconomic status. However, due to unforeseen circumstances, my financial situation had changed from those in my orbit of familiar people. The implication for my sons' futures was that they had to start supporting themselves immediately which included planning to secure a roof over their heads. Hence, their economic situation was no longer akin to that of people in their orbit of familiarity but comparable to that of many others in similar situations. In other words, their orbits of familiarity and similarity no longer overlapped.

Understanding and accepting our personal circumstances are the first steps towards achieving our life goals. They shift our thinking to focus on problem solving, a mindset so important without which one ends up dwelling on the past.

Chapter 2

Base Camp and the Two Peaks of Financial Independence

"As we equip you with the necessary information for your climb, let me describe Base Camp and the Two Peaks of Financial Independence", I said to my sons during our talk.

This mountain has two peaks, the First Peak and the Summit. On your climb up, you will first reach Base Camp which is a staging area that climbers use to prepare for the next phase of their climb. So there are a total of three milestones in this expedition, namely the Base Camp, the First Peak and the Summit. Analogously, the three financial goals many people aspire to attain in life are:

Goal 1: *To be 'Debt-free with Homeownership'* (reaching 'Base Camp')

You should aim to fully own a home with no outstanding debt before your 55th birthday. To put the mountain analogy in perspective, Base Camp of Mount Everest is 5,380 meters above sea level while the Summit's height is 8,848 meters.[1,2] The trek to Base Camp obviously brings you closer to the First Peak and the Summit. Similarly the trail after homeownership continues in the same direction that will lead you to financial independence.

---

[1] Mx. Granger, "Everest Base Camp Trek" (Wikivoyage, June 1, 2020) www.wikivoyage.org

[2] Kim Ann Zimmermann, "Mount Everest: World's Highest Mountain" (Live Science, September 20, 2012) www.livescience.com

Goal 2: *Having a 'Minimum Retirement Savings'* (reaching the 'First Peak')

At this juncture, your retirement savings would be more than enough to cover your expected living expenses for the rest of your life. After retirement, although the usage of funds may be partially from the principal, considering your age at that point of time, you would not be expected to outlive your savings. Reaching the 'First Peak' which is a significant achievement ensures that you will not be dependent on anyone for your living expenses and hence you will be financially secure.

Goal 3: *Having 'Full Retirement Savings'* (reaching the 'Summit')

At this point, the return from your retirement savings (passive income[3]) would be enough to cover expected living expenses for the rest of your life without drawing on the principal amount. Reaching the 'Summit' ensures that you will have significant funds to pass down.

While building up a 'minimum retirement savings' is a necessary goal to aspire to, achieving 'full retirement savings' is but an ideal for many of us. It is important to recognize your inherent goals of *financial security*[4] and work towards achieving them before your income diminishes significantly. Your employment related income will start to diminish at some point in your career and you will not be working during the tail end of your life. Hence, while you are in your 'income generating years', it is vital to pace your climb towards 'Base Camp and the Two Peaks of Financial Independence'.

---

[3] Passive income includes regular earnings from a source other than an employer. Passive income can come from two sources: rental property or a business in which one does not actively participate, such as being paid book royalties or stock dividends. James Royal, "11 passive income ideas to help you make money in 2020" bankrate.com (May 19, 2020) https://www.bankrate.com/investing/passive-income-ideas/

[4] Financial security refers to the peace of mind you feel when you aren't worried about your income being enough to cover your expenses. It also means that you have enough money saved to cover emergencies and your future financial goals. Quicken (2020) https://www.quicken.com/what-financial-security

Milestones

"With each success, I gain more confidence", words of wisdom from a young adult when he shared his feelings about successfully closing his first few deals at work.

You should identify milestones along your financial journey as they serve as interim objectives and indicate that you are on the right track and getting closer to the goal, hence motivating you to push on. As the 'climb' can be arduous, you will need periodic reassurances to encourage you along the journey.

Airlift

Some of you may be fortunate enough to be airlifted to 'Base Camp' by a helicopter. That is to say, you may come to own a property by virtue of a gift from your parents or by inheritance. If this is the case, then set your sights immediately on the next goal, the 'First Peak'.

The quest to be financially secure is actually inherent in all of us. According to Maslow's Hierarchy of Needs, humans need security in the form of 'shelter from the elements' and the 'necessities of life' to live, all of which come with costs.[5] The people we depend on while growing up, will pass on. Hence, ensuring we have a 'roof over our heads' and a livelihood without depending on anyone else is fundamental to our existence.

---

[5] Saul McLeod, "Maslow's Hierarchy of Needs" (Simply Psychology, March 20, 2020) https://www.simplypsychology.org/maslow.html

Base Camp and the Two Peaks

Figure 2.1: "Hiking to Everest Base Camp" by Kreete Tokman, Universal Traveller (May 10, 2018) https://www.universaltraveller.com.au/blog/5-things-no-one-tells-you-about-hiking-to-everest-base-camp

Chapter 3

Financial Health Dashboard

Financial Literacy

The Rosetta stone is a granodiorite stele inscribed with a decree issued in Egypt in 196 BCE and rediscovered in 1799. Due to the fact that the decree was inscribed thrice in different scripts and languages, the Rosetta stone served as the key to deciphering Egyptian hieroglyphs, thereby opening a window into ancient Egyptian history.[6]

Analogously, the key to deciphering financial transactions is The Accounting Equation which represents the relationship between the Assets, Liabilities and Equity of a person or business. It is the foundation for all financial transactions. The Accounting Equation enables us to understand the mechanics of financial transactions. Hence, in order to manage your personal financial health effectively, you should have a basic understanding of the 'Rosetta Stone of Financial Literacy'.

Components of any transaction can be classified as an Asset or a Liability. In the context of personal finance, the key terms are defined as follows:

- Asset is 'what you have'
- Liability is 'what you owe'
- Equity is 'the value you own'

---

[6] The British Museum, "Everything you wanted to know about the Rosetta Stone" (July 14, 2017) https://blog.britishmuseum.org/everything-you-ever-wanted-to-know-about-the-rosetta-stone/

The Accounting Equation is:

Asset = Liability + Equity

The left hand side of the equation shows 'what you have' (an asset).

The right hand side of the equation shows how you paid for the purchase of the asset, reflected as a liability for debt and as equity for the value you actually own.

You may obtain an asset by way of a purchase or receive it as a gift. If you received an asset as a gift, your liability for that asset is zero in which case, you fully own the asset.

Equity = Asset - Liability

Equity is the same as Net Worth which is a measure of your wealth.

Hence,

Net Worth = Total Assets - Total Liabilities

Let us assume that growing up; you accumulated savings from various sources such as gifts for special occasions and income from summer jobs. With no debt whatsoever, you currently have S$5,000 in your savings account and are about to start your first job.

Your financial position can be viewed as follows:

Asset (Savings S$5,000) = Liability (S$0) + Equity (S$5,000)

Equity (S$5,000) = Asset (S$5,000) - Liability (S$0)

Net Worth = S$5,000

As a personal reward for landing your first job, you bought yourself a new laptop priced at S$2,000.

The various ways by which you could have paid for the purchase are illustrated below along with your financial position after each possible transaction.

Case 1: You paid S$2,000 in cash from your savings.

Financial position:

Net Worth = Asset (Laptop S$2,000 + Savings S$3,000) - Liability (S$0)

Net Worth = S$5,000

Case 2: You paid S$1,000 in cash from your savings and borrowed S$1,000 from your older sister to pay the balance amount. You have to return the loan in 1 year with interest. She charges interest to inculcate in you the value of money.

Financial position:

Net Worth = Asset (Laptop S$2,000 + Savings S$4,000) - Liability (S$1,000)

Net Worth = S$5,000

Case 3: You paid S$1,000 in cash from your savings and the balance amount of S$1,000 was paid by your parents as a gift.

Financial position:

Net Worth = Asset (Laptop S$2,000 + Savings S$4,000) - Liability (S$0)

Net Worth = S$6,000

Case 4: Your parents paid the entire amount of S$2,000 as a gift.

Financial position:

Net Worth = Asset (Laptop S$2,000 + Savings S$5,000) - Liability (S$0)

Net Worth = S$7,000

Your Net Worth is basically your wealth which is the value of your assets at a given point of time minus your liabilities. The Accounting Equation shows a snapshot of your financial position on a particular day. Your Net Worth would be different after a period of time. Without taking into account other sources of cash inflow and outflow, let's see what your Net Worth would look like in Cases 1 and 2 after one year.

Assumption: The interest rate on your savings account is 1% per year.

Case 1 after 1 year: (You paid S$2,000 in cash from your savings.)

Due to wear and tear, the value of the Laptop after 1 year is S$1,600. Your savings of S$3,000 earns an interest of 1% per annum which is S$30.

Financial position:

Net Worth = Assets (Laptop S$1,600 + Savings S$3,030) - Liabilities (0)

Net Worth = S$4,630

Case 2 after 1 year: (You paid S$1,000 in cash from your savings and borrowed S$1,000 from your older sister to pay the balance amount. You have to return the loan in 1 year with interest.)

Due to wear and tear, the value of the Laptop after 1 year is S$1,600. Your sister charges an interest rate of 10% per annum payable with the principal amount. Your interest expense incurred on your loan of S$1,000 is S$100. You pay her the total amount of S$1,100 from your savings. Your savings of S$4,000 earns an interest of 1% per annum which is S$40.

Financial position:

Net Worth = Assets (Laptop S$1,600 + Savings S$4,040) - Liabilities (S$1,100)

Net Worth = Assets (Laptop S$1,600 + Savings S$2,940) - Liabilities (S$0)

Net Worth = S$4,540

So although your laptop in both Case 1 and Case 2 has the same value after one year, your Net Worth would be less in Case 2, that is if you borrowed to pay for your purchase which incurs an additional cost by way of interest on the loan.

The interest rate on loans is always higher than the interest rate on savings. This is how banks make money, paying a low interest on our savings and lending us money at higher interest rates.

Case 2B

Building on the example of Case 2, assume that your gross salary is S$3,000 per month. After a provident fund[7] deduction of S$600, your net pay is S$2,400 per month. Your monthly expenses are estimated to average S$1,500 per month. Hence, you can save S$900 when you receive your pay each month. Assuming an interest rate of 1% per annum compounded monthly, in one year, your new savings balance would be S$13,990 (rounded to the nearest integer).[8]

---

[7] A provident fund is a retirement fund run by the government. They are generally compulsory, often through taxes, and are funded by both employer and employee contributions.– Troy Segal, "Provident Fund vs. Pension Fund" (Investopedia, July 20, 2020)
https://www.investopedia.com/ask/answers/102814/what-are-main-differences-between-provident-fund-and-pension-fund.asp
[8] "How Often Is Interest Accrued on a Savings Account?" (The Motley Fool, Aug. 24, 2017)
https://www.fool.com/saving/how-often-is-interest-accrued-on-a-savings-account.aspx

Table 3.1: Monthly Compounding Interest Calculation Example (S$)

				Interest rate per annum		1.00%
Month	Saving	B/F	Beginning Balance	Interest	Ending Balance
					4,000
1		4,000	4,000	3.33	4,003
2	900	4,003	4,903	4.09	4,907
3	900	4,907	5,807	4.84	5,812
4	900	5,812	6,712	5.59	6,718
5	900	6,718	7,618	6.35	7,624
6	900	7,624	8,524	7.10	8,531
7	900	8,531	9,431	7.86	9,439
8	900	9,439	10,339	8.62	10,348
9	900	10,348	11,248	9.37	11,257
10	900	11,257	12,157	10.13	12,167
11	900	12,167	13,067	10.89	13,078
12	900	13,078	13,978	11.65	13,990
			Total	89.82	

In Case 2B, the monthly contribution to savings (S$900 x 11 months) and the total interest earned on savings (S$90) are inflows added to your cash asset. The loan (S$1,000) and interest (S$100) payable are liabilities which once paid, are reflected as cash outflows, hence reducing your cash asset.

Financial position:

Beginning of year:

Net Worth = Assets (Laptop S$2,000 + Savings S$4,000) - Liabilities (S$1,000)

Net Worth = S$5,000

End of year (before repaying the loan and interest):

Net Worth = Assets (Laptop S$1,600 + Savings S$13,990) - Liabilities (S$1,100)

Net Worth = S$14,490

End of year (after repaying the loan and interest, i.e. S$13,990 - S$1,000 - S$100):

Net Worth = Assets (Laptop S$1,600 + Savings S$12,890) - Liabilities (S$0)

Net Worth = S$14,490

In your savings account statement, the 'end of year' amount of S$12,890 is then 'carried forward' (C/F) to the following period. In the next statement, the balance 'brought forward' (B/F) from the previous period becomes the 'beginning of year' balance of the new period.

Unlike a company which is required by law to record and keep evidence of every transaction, we as individuals do not consistently maintain such detailed records of our expenses. Nevertheless, the difference between the beginning and ending balances in our accounts essentially factors in the total inflow and the total outflow of cash, hence accounting for the change in Net worth (NW).

From Case 2B,

Net worth Change = NW at end of year - NW at beginning of year

Net Worth Change = S$14,490 - S$5,000

Net Worth Change = S$9,490

In this case, Net Worth change came from monthly savings (positive change) and depreciation of the laptop (negative change).

Asset value loss = S$400 (laptop is worth less after 1 year)

For personal finance, depreciating assets like laptops and other consumer goods should be considered as expenses and left out of your asset list. Such items lose their market value substantially within 3 to 5 years.

Assets can appreciate or depreciate in value over time. For example, if a property is worth more since the time of purchase, the property has appreciated in value. On the other hand, cars lose their worth over time due to wear and tear, hence depreciate in value. An increase in value of an asset increases Net Worth and vice versa. An increase or decrease in an asset's value is known as Capital Gain or Capital Loss respectively. Other examples of personal assets increasing or decreasing in value are gold and shares in a business. Hence your Net Worth can increase from an accumulation of savings as well as from Capital Gain on your assets. However, capital gain on an asset can be just on paper unless it is realized (monetized) by a sale of the asset.

Financial Health Dashboard

A financial health dashboard provides an overall snapshot of your wealth at a specific period in time. It is a summary of your assets (what you own), your liabilities (what you owe), and your net worth (assets minus liabilities).

Tabulate your assets and liabilities at the end of each calendar year and compare your Net Worth at the beginning and end of the year. The difference in your Net Worth depicts the change in your wealth after one year.

Net Worth = Total Assets minus Total Liabilities

Classify your assets as follows:

Personal Assets

- Cash (or e-wallet)[9]
- Savings & Investments
- Savings in Provident fund
- Home (current property value)

Personal Liabilities

- Home Loan (outstanding amount)
- Other bills payable (if any)

---

[9] "eWallet is an online prepaid account used to store money and transact online and offline through a computer or a smartphone whenever required."- Aashish Pahwa, "eWallet-Everything you should know about Prepaid Wallets" (Feeddough.com, Aug.19, 2019) https://www.feedough.com/e-wallet/

Table 3.2: Financial Health Dashboard Example (S$)

Assets	Beginning of year	End of year	Change
Cash or e-wallet	100	500	400
Savings	4,000	12,890	8,890
Provident fund	0	12,424	12,424
Home (property)	0	0	0
Total Assets (A)	4,100	25,814	21,714
Liabilities			
Payables	1,000	0	-1,000
Home Loan	0	0	0
Total Liabilities (L)	1,000	0	-1,000
Net Worth (A-L)	3,100	25,814	22,714

Net Worth beginning of year = S$3,100

Net Worth end of year = S$25,814

Net Worth Change = S$22,714

If you are employed in Singapore, the current rate of contributions to the Central Provident Fund is 20% of salary by the employee and 17% of salary by the employer.[10] The interest rates are tiered according to account categories and amounts. The provident fund figure in the table above is based on an average interest rate of 3.5%. The provident fund is part of your overall savings and hence you should include it in your 'financial health dashboard'.

The only 'big ticket' item I have listed above as an asset is property. Automobiles and other durable goods depreciate in value due to 'wear and tear' and hence they are basically expensed annually over several years with a low 'salvage value'[11]. However, if you purchase a durable good such as an automobile on loan, then you must include it in your asset list and the corresponding outstanding loan as a liability. My personal recommendation is that if you need or want to own a car, buy one that you can afford to pay for in cash. Perhaps you can start with a pre-owned (used) car which is less expensive than a new car. It is part of 'living within your means'. Furthermore, the interest portions on car loans work out higher because of the method of calculation used. Unlike a home loan where interest is calculated on the monthly outstanding loan, an auto loan comes with the total interest on the full value of the loan which is added to the initial loan value. The sum is then divided by the payment period to derive the monthly instalment amount.

---

[10] Central Provident Fund Board, Singapore
https://www.cpf.gov.sg/Employers/EmployerGuides/employer-guides/paying-cpf-contributions/cpf-contribution-and-allocation-rates
[11] Salvage Value is the estimated resale value of an asset at the end of its useful life.

Table 3.3: Car Loan Instalment Calculation Example (S$)

Term (years)	5	(A)
Interest rate (per annum)	3%	(B)
Loan Amount	90,000	(C)
Total interest	13,500	(D=A*B*C)
Total loan+interest	103,500	(X=C+D)
Monthly instalment	1,725	(Y=X/60)

In addition to depreciation and fuel costs, other expenses related to owning a car are annual registration, insurance, maintenance and repairs. Increasingly popular are car leasing schemes where you return the car after several years for a new one. In either case, you would need to factor the expenses into your budget.

Your home will probably be the biggest part of your wealth. An investment asset may need to be sold for a variety of reasons, whereas you will always need a 'roof over your head' no matter what the circumstances. Therefore, once you have completed the mortgage payments for your home, I recommend removing it from your asset list when monitoring your financial health dashboard.

Figure 3.1: Components that impact Net Worth

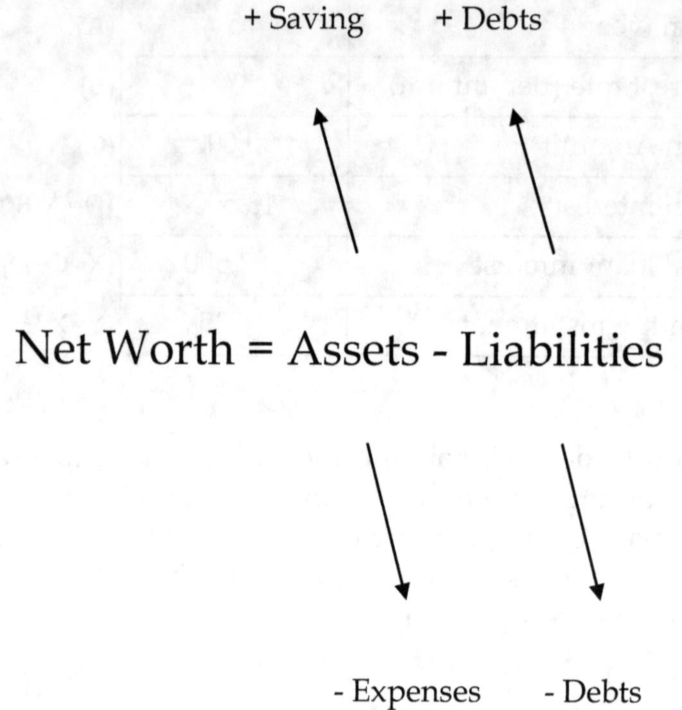

- Saving increases cash assets, hence increasing net worth
- Expenses reduces cash assets, hence reducing net worth
- Increasing debts add to liabilities, hence reducing net worth
- Reducing debts decreases liabilities, hence increasing net worth

'Net Worth at end of year' minus 'Net Worth at beginning of year'

= 'Wealth Creation' or 'Wealth Loss' for the year

Chapter 4

Homeownership or Home Savings?

As mentioned in Chapter 2, humans need security in the form of 'shelter from the elements' (roof over our heads) and the 'necessities of life' to sustain our livelihood, all of which come with costs. No land is without ownership and hence we cannot expect to pitch a tent on any vacant land. Properties are owned by private citizens, organisations or the state. We cannot even grow our own produce for food except on property we own. So the security of these two basic needs of life (shelter and food) is naturally a priority for all of us before we can pursue other needs and wants in life.

Homeownership

Owning a home does not necessarily mean living in the property you own. You could be living in a rented place because of proximity to work or you may be living with your parents for various reasons. Nevertheless you should consider owning a property that you may eventually end up living in, especially during your 'non income generating years' and the 'tail end of your life'.

If you are fortunate enough to fulfil this goal of homeownership by way of a gift or inheritance, then target the next goal of financial independence, namely having a 'minimum retirement savings'. Otherwise you need a plan that puts you on the path towards homeownership. Due to significant costs of properties compared to the average personal income, you may need a runway of up to 25 years to fully own a property while maintaining your lifestyle. In most countries, the maximum mortgage loan term[12] is calculated by subtracting the current age of the applicant from the general retirement age. For example, if the general retirement age in your country is set at age 60 and you are 35 years old at the time of application, the maximum mortgage term would be 25 years. Furthermore, since mortgage loans are mostly capped at 90% of the property value, you have to save up for the balance of the value plus for furniture and interior decorations. Hence, it is necessary to start saving for the equity portion several years before you expect to purchase the property.

Your source of income would generally be from remuneration if you are a working professional or from profits if you are an entrepreneur. In both cases, there are external uncertainties. If you run a business, you are exposed to the conditions of the market in which you operate. If you are a working professional, the market sets a time limit for your employment period primarily guided by the official retirement age. Although the average life expectancy of humans has increased significantly, the physical and mental effects of the ageing process weigh down on a person's ability to compete with younger workers, thus leading to potentially diminishing income as a person gets older. The window of one's prime earning years (most productive years) is limited and hence the case to plan early in your career. The relationship between age and potential earning ability can be generalized as depicted in the table below.

---

[12] A mortgage is a loan in which property is used as collateral.

Table 4.1: Relationship between 'Age range' and 'Earning ability'

Age range	Earning ability
24 to 39 years old	Prime earning years
40 to 45 years old	Risk of redundancy unless one assumes increased job responsibility and/or one's skill sets are in demand
46-55 years old	Higher risk of redundancy due to legacy costs to company
56-63 years old	Potential candidate for forced retirement / difficult to get a new job due to older age
64 years & above	Very limited options for employment

At the risk of sounding pessimistic, one's income could be disrupted by an unexpected disability. While payout from a typical disability insurance may cover living expenses, it would not be sufficient to pay for rent and hence the case to fully own a home as a hedge against any loss of income due to serious illness.

Considering your prime earning years of 15 years and another 15 years of possibly increasing risk to your income stream, you should set a deadline to fully own your home before you turn 55 years old. Factoring in time, let's say 5 years, to save up for the equity portion of the purchase and 25 years for the mortgage loan period, you practically have to start saving when you are 25 years old or as you start on your first job. The arithmetic is:

55 years old - 25 year loan - 5 years of saving = 25 years old

While my explanation of when to start planning for your own home may seem obvious, it is not a priority for most single young adults in their first year of work. This leads to a misrepresentation of their disposable income as their budgets may not include home savings as an item. Furthermore, this oversight is often because young adults may still be living with their parents.

Some of the reasons young adults leave the nest are the desire for independence, need for personal privacy, need for more physical space or even to avoid disharmony within the family. These are actually triggers that may eventually lead to purchasing your own home but they are not reasons. You should aim to fully own a home even if you are living with an extended family for the reason of achieving financial security.

There was a time when most people waited until the end of their careers to buy a home with their savings. Today, with widespread availability of consumer credit, property prices tend to increase significantly over time due to factors such as urbanization, limited land space and the impact of globalization. So depending on your level of income and choice of home location, your savings may not be enough to buy a property at the end of your career. Hence, you would likely be locking in the price by buying a home early in your career while you are still eligible for a mortgage loan.

Home Savings

Some of you may prefer not to have a mortgage debt, especially if you have the option of living with your parents. In this case, you should build up a home savings amount equivalent to the cost of owning a home. Unless you are gifted with or inherit a home, adequate home savings will be a safety net for rent when you do not have active income in later years. Perhaps you will decide to purchase a home in cash with your home savings funds when you retire.

If you are living on your own and paying rent because you prefer not to have a mortgage debt, then I would advise to also consider that rent is an expense while a mortgage payment is a payment towards ownership. Furthermore, unlike a personal loan or credit card debt, which I am against, a mortgage loan is a secured loan specifically tied to a property. Nevertheless, you must have a regular and stable income stream to ensure timely payment of the mortgage instalments.

Chapter 5

Action Plan

"A goal without a plan is just a wish" - Antoine de Saint-Exupéry

As the quote above suggests, you should have an action plan that lays out a path towards achieving your financial security goals. Several key steps are outlined below:

Step 1: Prepare a Budget

Step 2: Organise your bank accounts into 4 categories (Chapter 6)

Step 3: Prepare a Cash Assets Projection (Chapter 7)

Step 4: Set specific objectives to attain your goals and identify interim milestones

Step 5: Monitor your progress

Step 1 of Action Plan: Prepare a Budget

A budget is an estimate of income and expenses for a set period of time. Having a budget does not imply that you have to forgo things you desire. On the contrary, preparing a budget helps you to plan for the things you desire in life. A budget reminds you how to allocate portions of your monthly pay cheque based on priorities that you have already considered and decided on. Monitoring your expenses on a monthly basis to compare with your budget and if necessary, making adjustments to your spending habits will help you stay on track towards achieving your goals. So for your budget, set the period of time as monthly and group your expenses into four categories, namely

A) Rent or Home Loan Payment or Home Savings

B) Living Expenses

C) Savings for Financial Security

D) Provision for Contributions Fund (Charity)

A)-Rent, Home Loan Payment or Home Savings

Even if you are living under your parents' roof at no rental charge, allocate this expense in your budget and transfer into a 'home savings' account at the beginning of each month as though you are paying rent or a home loan instalment. These funds are to be used for the equity portion of your future home purchase or to build up adequate 'home savings' as a safety net.

It can be assumed that on average, home rental rates tend to be similar to home loan instalments (depending on the debt to equity ratio of the purchase financing). So instead of paying rent, you may want to consider paying down a home loan and eventually own the property. Additionally, after many years, should you decide to 'downsize' your living space and sell the property, the likely capital gain can be a very useful contribution to your retirement fund.

B)-Living Expenses

Itemize your living expenses as follows:

- Home maintenance fees (if you own a property)
- Home insurance (if you own a property)
- Utilities
- Internet service subscriptions
- Food & beverage
- Transportation (including maintenance and repair costs if you own a vehicle)
- Mobile phone charges
- Insurance - (hospitalization & surgery; life insurance if you have dependents)
- Entertainment
- Holiday trips
- Miscellaneous
- Student loan instalment (if any)

If you are living with your parents, it is likely that you can save not only on rent but also on some of the living expenses listed above. Nevertheless, you should allocate these expenses in your budget and transfer the amount saved to a 'home savings' account. Note that some of the expenses such as holiday trips and insurance are usually incurred once a year. For a monthly budget, you should divide any annual expense by 12 to get the prorated amount.

Shape your lifestyle according to your income level; live within your means without having to borrow to meet your expenses. To help you control your expenses, understand what you need versus what you want.

Needs versus Wants

A 'need' is something you have to have to survive or complete a task.

A 'want' is simply the desire for something, not necessary for survival (e.g. goods that are "nice to have").

Before purchasing an item, always determine whether something is a 'need' or a 'want'. A tip to help decide is to wait at least a week before purchasing the item. Having said that, it is perfectly reasonable to desire and purchase a luxury item as long as you have budgeted for it. To think that you can afford it can be deceiving because you may not have factored in other expenses or allocations towards meeting your financial goals. So preparing a budget would help to ensure that you do not miss out on things that are inherently more important to you.

Miscellaneous

Any other living expenses not mentioned in the list can also be itemized or even grouped under miscellaneous.

Student Loan

Personally, I feel that all young adults should start their career debt-free which implies that their education costs up to tertiary level should be the responsibility of their parents and the government. However, not all parents can afford this and many students therefore take student loans. If you have a student loan debt, then ensure to include it in your budget and itemize it separately.

Insurance

Insurance is an arrangement with a company to guarantee compensation for specified loss, damage, illness or death in return for a specified premium. Your savings may not be enough to cover expenses that may be incurred due to an unexpected event, hence the need to ensure adequate coverage. In other words, insurance policies cover 'what if' scenarios. 'What if' questions to ask yourself are:

1) What if I fall sick and get hospitalized?
2) What if I fall sick and need surgery?
3) What if my illness requires prolonged medical treatment?
4) What if, because of my illness or an accident, I can no longer work?
5) Do I have family members who depend on my income? Who will provide for them if I pass away?
6) What if I am temporarily unemployed and have no income to pay for my monthly expenses?

For scenarios 1 to 3, you need to purchase *health insurance* to cover hospitalization, surgery and treatment, expenses which can be very costly. Depending on which country you live in, health insurance may be legally mandated, in which case you have to buy a policy. In some countries, health care costs are covered by government health systems such as the National Health Service in the United Kingdom. Health insurance premiums go up over time with age. Furthermore, if you are aged sixty years and above, buying a new health insurance policy will come with more restrictive terms, especially around the issue of pre-existing conditions. "A medical illness or injury that you have before you start a new health care plan may be considered a pre-existing condition."[13] Hence, ensure your health insurance policy is valid before you turn 60 years old, so that at the end of the term, the existing policy can be renewed without disruption.

For scenario 4, you need to purchase *disability insurance*. If you become disabled due to an accident or illness and are unable to work, you will not have income to cover your monthly expenses. Disability insurance will provide monthly payouts to cover basic living expenses. However, note that while such payouts may cover your basic living expenses, it would probably not be enough to cover rent or home loan instalments.

For scenario 5, that is if you have family members who are dependent on your income, you need to purchase a *life insurance* policy. In the event that you pass away, the beneficiaries stated in the policy will receive a lump sum amount. Hence, the amount to insure should be enough to provide for your dependents' needs until they become independent. The purpose of a life insurance is so that your dependents are not saddled with debt such as mortgage payments and can continue to pay for basic living expenses including health insurance premiums and education expenses.

---

[13] "What is a Pre-Existing Condition?" (Cigna, July 2018)
https://www.cigna.com/individuals-families/understanding-insurance/what-is-a-pre-existing-condition

Minimum Savings Amount (Emergency fund)

For scenario 6, the only insurance coverage for such a situation is to have enough savings. So how much is enough? It depends on how soon you can find another job, and this depends on the general job market trend and your employability. On average, it can take between six to twelve months to land a job depending on the state of the economy. Hence, you should build up and always maintain savings of no less than twelve months' worth of your monthly expenses. This 'Minimum Savings Amount' must not be invested in any assets because it is your reserve fund to meet your monthly expenses in case you find yourself unemployed and without an income stream. It can be deposited in a fixed savings account which will provide a slightly higher interest rate than a regular savings account.

Note: Your Central Provident Fund (CPF) account should not be a substitute for the 'minimum savings amount' fund because you are not allowed to withdraw from CPF accounts except for certain specified purposes.

Home Insurance

If you own a home, you need to cover against loss due to damage of property in case of a fire with a *fire insurance* policy. In fact, your mortgage bank will require such a policy as part of the loan contract while the property is still mortgaged to them. You may also consider insurance for loss of personal belongings due to a fire. Another type of insurance is *burglary insurance* which covers loss of personal belongings due to burglary. In some countries, depending on the local environment, it may be advisable to insure against damages incurred by natural disasters such as floods and earthquakes.

C)-Savings for Financial Security

From your monthly pay cheque, a fixed amount should be saved into a separate savings account at the beginning of each month. The purpose of this account is to build up adequate funds for your financial security. A suitable amount can be determined after factoring in estimates of your other expenses. While savings is technically not an expense, the allocation and transfer should be done monthly as part of the monthly cash outflow. Do not wait to see what is leftover at the end of the month. It should be treated as an expense and hence transferred just after receiving your pay cheque. This is a way to practise self-discipline.

Saving money means to set aside a part of your income for future use. Savings do not have a significant risk of loss because it is usually deposited in a savings account with a bank for an 'almost risk-free' return called interest. Financial institutions such as banks insure savings deposits up to a certain amount to protect against claims by depositors in case of bankruptcy.[14] Yes, banks can fail just like any other business.

Saving is investing without risk. Saving is prudent. Prudence provides stability.

---

[14] "In the event of a Deposit Insurance Scheme member bank or finance company failing, all of your insured deposits with that member are aggregated and insured up to S$75,000 by the Singapore Deposit Insurance Corporation Limited (SDIC)" "Deposit Insurance Scheme", (SDIC, 2019) https://www.sdic.org.sg/

D)-Provision for Contributions Fund (Charity/Filial Piety/Pay it forward)

"Charity begins at home" - Sir Thomas Browne

A nominal amount from your monthly pay cheque should be allocated for future contributions to charitable causes. The amount should not compromise your ability to fulfil the other components of your monthly expenses. The provision should be monthly, thus allowing time for gradual accumulation. Again, I stress that the monthly allocation should be nominal without affecting your own journey to achieving your financial goals.

As the quote above suggests, your first responsibility is for the needs of your family. Hence, potential beneficiaries of your charity fund could be your parents; a family member in serious need; a friend in need; a charity organisation or a worthy cause. You do not have to decide on the beneficiaries immediately but allocate and build up a separate fund so that when needed, you can contribute without affecting your other commitments and savings. If you lend money to a needy person from the fund, you could write-off the loan in case of default without ill feelings as the purpose of the fund is to pay it forward.

Table 5.1: Monthly Budget Example (S$)

			2,200	3,000
		Monthly Gross Salary	2,200	3,000
		Provident Fund deduction	440	600
		Other deductions	0	0
		Net Pay Cheque	1,760	2,400
1)	Transfer to Savings (financial security fund)		400	800
2)	Rent	If you are living with	400	600
3)	Utilities	your parents, transfer to	50	50
4)	Internet subscription	'home savings account'	35	35
5)	Food & Beverage		450	450
6)	Transport		120	120
7)	Mobile phone charges		20	20
8)	Insurance			
	-hospitalization & surgery	Prorated	20	20
	-life (if you have dependents)		0	0
9)	Entertainment		100	100
10)	Holiday trips	Prorated	80	100
11)	Miscellaneous		60	60
12)	Student loan instalment (if any)		0	0
13)	Provision for Contributions (charity/filial piety/pay it forward)		25	45
		Total	1,760	2,400

Table 5.2: Monthly Transfers into 4 Separate Accounts Example (S$)

A/C 1	General fund - to receive salary and for daily transactions	In/Out	In/Out
A/C 2	Home Savings fund - for future home	485	685
A/C 3	Savings - for financial security	400	800
A/C 4	Provision for Contribution fund	25	45

Compound Interest

Compound interest is the addition of interest to the principal sum of a deposit, or in other words, it includes interest on interest. Depending on the type of savings account, interest is calculated and paid at different intervals. There are few methods of compounding interest that are commonly used:

- Annual compounding: Interest is calculated and paid once a year
- Quarterly compounding: Interest is calculated and paid once every three months
- Monthly compounding: Interest is calculated and paid each month
- Daily compounding: Interest is calculated and paid every day

So if you refrain from spending the interest earned, your money will grow, even in a savings account.[15]

Compounding Interest Calculation Example

Assumption: A 2-year 'fixed savings deposit' interest rate of 3.5% per annum, monthly compounding and beginning principal amount of S$13,990.

---

[15] "How Often Is Interest Accrued on a Savings Account?" (The Motley Fool, Aug. 24, 2017)
https://www.fool.com/saving/how-often-is-interest-accrued-on-a-savings-account.aspx

Table 5.3: Monthly Compounding Interest Calculation Example (S$)

	Interest rate per annum:	3.50%	
Month	Beginning Bal.	Interest	Ending Balance
B/F			13,990
1	13,990	41	14,031
2	14,031	41	14,072
3	14,072	41	14,113
4	14,113	41	14,154
5	14,154	41	14,195
6	14,195	41	14,237
7	14,237	42	14,278
8	14,278	42	14,320
9	14,320	42	14,362
10	14,362	42	14,403
11	14,403	42	14,445
12	14,445	42	14,488
13	14,488	42	14,530
14	14,530	42	14,572
15	14,572	43	14,615
16	14,615	43	14,657
17	14,657	43	14,700
18	14,700	43	14,743
19	14,743	43	14,786
20	14,786	43	14,829
21	14,829	43	14,872
22	14,872	43	14,916
23	14,916	44	14,959
24	14,959	44	15,003
	Total	1,013	

Investing

To invest means to buy an asset with the expectation that your investment will make higher returns. There is a risk of losing your money depending on the type of asset purchased. Simply put, the downside of a business is that it can become unprofitable or even fail, thus destroying the value of the ownership. Of course, on the flip side, the returns can be quite rewarding if the business is profitable. Why the value of a business increases or decreases is not within an investor's control. Hence all investments come with varying degrees of risk, bankruptcy being the worst-case scenario.

So investments should only be considered once your monthly expenses are being comfortably serviced and after having built up a 'minimum savings amount'. Even after meeting these conditions, you must be mentally prepared for the possibility of your investment losing value due to situations beyond your control.

An important point to note is that personal investments must be funded from savings (not from loans) with the possible exception of property assets. This is because if you use loans to invest and if the value of the invested asset falls below the loan amount, you will lose money as you have to top up the difference to cover the lost value of the investment. Such an event is called a 'margin call' which is a major reason why investors are forced to sell their assets at steep discounts.

Trading is not investing

Trading is buying and selling an asset for short term profit. Trading is a business activity which requires up to date and real-time knowledge of the market and hence full time attention is needed.

On the other hand, investing is done for long term gain with a focus on the fundamental strength of an asset to generate returns in the long run. If you are not a full time trader by profession, then do not trade.

What is the logic of investing? Do you need to jump on the bandwagon? Obviously we need to accumulate money because we 'consume' money when we pay for necessities and other living expenses. An honest way to accumulate money is to save from your income. As the price of goods and services tend to increase every year (inflation), your savings may buy you a little less of what you could buy a year earlier because savings account interest rates are almost always lower than the inflation rate. The desire to make up for this slight loss in future value of money is what motivates people to take risks, knowingly or unknowingly, and invest in businesses. Note that prices of goods and services can also fall (deflation) which happens due to oversupply, weak demand or even a complete stop in demand due to unexpected catastrophic events such as a pandemic. In such times, your savings can buy you more of what you could buy a year earlier.

If your income is stable for a good part of your career, you can accumulate substantial savings without having to take the risk of investing in other assets. On the other hand, having substantial savings enables you to allocate part of your savings for investments. So when you are financially stable and if you do get the itch to dip your toes in the world of investing, then here are some preconditions and rules to note before you part with your hard earned savings.

1) Has your savings reached the 'Minimum Savings Amount' (Emergency fund)?

You do not want to be caught without reserves in an emergency and be forced to sell your assets in a hurry at a discount. Even if this condition is met, do not use up all the rest of your savings for investing.

2) Assess the stability and sustainability of your source of income. Is your job relatively secure? If you are self-employed, is your business profitable?

3) Assess your pending and upcoming commitments such as mortgage loan and dependents' expenses (education, medical copayments[16] provision).

4) Ensure that you and your dependents have adequate health insurance coverage because treatment for a serious illness can be very costly.

5) Assess your risk appetite and temperament. Do you tend to feel a surge of anxiety when faced with a stressful situation? Adverse situations can affect your health due to stress.

6) Are you investing in your own business and managing yourself? If so, ensure to separate your personal budget from your business budget. Know when to cut your losses before your livelihood gets affected.

7) If you are investing as a sleeping partner, is the managing partner personally known to you? Do you trust your partner? How will you benefit from the investment?

8) If you are investing in a publicly listed company, remind yourself that the company Income Statement is also called a Profit and Loss Statement. As the title of the document suggests, sometimes the company can make a profit and sometimes it can make a loss.

---

[16] Copayment is a fixed amount that you have to pay over and above the deductible stipulated in your health insurance policy.

Investments are purchases of assets, namely ownership in businesses (equities), properties, commodities, precious metals and debt instruments like bonds[17]. The various market exchanges such as stock (or equity) markets are literally markets that match buyers and sellers of assets. One does not invest in a market; the investments are in assets such as partial ownership in companies with share certificates (or scripts) as official receipts of the purchases. It is important to understand this fact so that your decisions are made objectively. Think of the attractiveness of a business based on the demand for its product and the competence of the management to deliver results. This is an important mindset to have when investing; the alternative would be simply 'following the herd'.

Rule of 72

The rule of 72 is a mathematical method for estimating an investment's doubling time.[18] The rule number 72 is divided by the interest percentage per period (usually a year) to obtain the approximate number of periods required for doubling.

Years to double = 72 / Interest rate

Interest can also be the rate of return on an investment.

Example 1: If the annual compounded interest rate is 4%, then:

Years to double = 72 / 4 = 18 years

---

[17] When an investor purchases a bond, they are 'loaning' that money (called the principal) to the bond issuer, which is usually raising money for some project.

[18] Caroline Banton, The Rule of 72 Defined (Investopedia, June 20, 2019) https://www.investopedia.com/ask/answers/what-is-the-rule-72/

Example 2: If the annual compounded interest rate is 6%, then:

Years to double = 72 / 6 = 12 years

However, all investments come with a risk that means you can lose money. Being in a hurry to grow your money can cause you to lose your hard earned money. A way to determine a reasonable risk level is to use the fixed savings deposit rate as a base and add 'alpha', the risk premium. Knowing that if compounded, your investment can double in 'X' years (depending on the rate of return), there is no need to aim for the sky as no life net can cushion your fall from dangerous heights.

Table 5.4: Rule of 72

Annual Interest Rate	Years to Double	
	The Rule of 72	Actual Number of Years
1%	72	69.66
2%	36	35.00
3%	24	23.45
4%	18	17.67
5%	14.4	14.21
6%	12	11.90
7%	10.29	10.24
8%	9	9.01
9%	8	8.04
10%	7.2	7.27

Retirement

It is counter-intuitive to think of retirement when you are a young adult and just starting to work. Many governments mandate some form of provident fund so that employees will have some savings upon retirement. Your first pay cheque amount is very likely a net amount after deduction for a provident fund. Hence it would make sense to question early on whether your provident fund savings will support your living after retirement.

Retirement, according to the dictionary, is to "withdraw from one's position or occupation or from active working life."[19] At some point in your life, either by choice or old age, you will be retired. As long as you are alive, there will be monthly expenses to be paid, namely living expenses which would include rent, if you don't own a home. Some expense items will likely be less but some like health insurance premiums will be higher.

Monthly Expenses after Retirement:

A) Rent, if you don't own a home

B) Living expenses

- Home maintenance fees
- Home insurance
- Utilities
- Internet subscription
- Food & beverage
- Transportation
- Mobile phone charges
- Entertainment

---

[19] Dana Anspach, "What Retirement Is and How to Get There" (the balance, March 2, 2020) https://www.thebalance.com/what-is-retirement-2388822

- Holiday trips
- Insurance - (hospitalization & surgery)
- Miscellaneous
- Caregiver
- Medicines

Having a look at the list of expense items above should indicate to you that you need a lump sum of money for retirement. The biggest item is rent and hence you should target to own your home before retirement. What should the 'minimum retirement amount' of savings be? This would depend on your living expenses according to your lifestyle, your health, the adequacy of your health insurance coverage and how long you are expected to live. It would be prudent to plan based on the median lifespan in your city. In Chapter 7, I have made cash assets projection until the age of 85 years.

Minimum Retirement Savings

A study conducted in 2019 by researchers in Singapore concluded that a single man or woman would need at least S$1,379 per month to meet basic living expenses.[20] Assuming that a young adult today retires at 68 years of age, the future value of S$1,379 today is about S$2,540 in 40 years at an inflation rate of 1.4%.

If one is expected to live at least until the age of 85 years, then in the absence of any other income after retirement at age 68 years, the minimum retirement amount should cover 17 years of living expenses.

S$2,540 x 12 months x 17 years = S$518,160

---

[20] Ng KH, Teo YY, Neo YW, Maulod A & Ting YT, "What older people need in Singapore: A household budgets study" (Lee Kuan Yew School of Public Policy, 2019) https://whatsenoughsg.files.wordpress.com/2019/05/what-older-people-need-in-singapore-a-household-budgets-study-full-report.pdf

Obviously the entire amount is not required at once and your savings continue to earn interest. Besides, you may have passive income from other investments. You may also decide to downsize your living space and cash in on the capital gain of your home which will add to your retirement savings. Furthermore, expenses are usually lower on a per person basis when household resources are shared. So the 'minimum retirement savings' is a range depending on individual circumstances.

Chapter 6

Bank Accounts Organisation

Step 2 of Action Plan: Organise your bank accounts into 4 categories

In order to help you maintain budget discipline and to monitor your progress, open 4 separate bank accounts for different purposes.

Account Category 1: General fund

> Purpose: To receive salary and conduct daily expense transactions

Account Category 2: Home Savings fund

> Purpose: To build up funds for a home purchase or home savings safety net

Account Category 3: Financial Security fund

> Purpose: To build up funds for financial security

Account Category 4: Provision for Contributions (Charity/Filial Piety)

Purpose: To build up funds for future charitable contributions

Apart from Account 1 (General fund), the three other accounts are to be treated as 'silos', that is you should not transfer between accounts as each has a specific purpose. However, once funds in Account 3 (Financial Security fund) have reached the 'minimum savings amount', any excess should be transferred to Account 2 (Home Savings fund) to build up enough savings for a down payment or for adequate home savings as a safety net.

Figure 6.1: Accounts Organisation

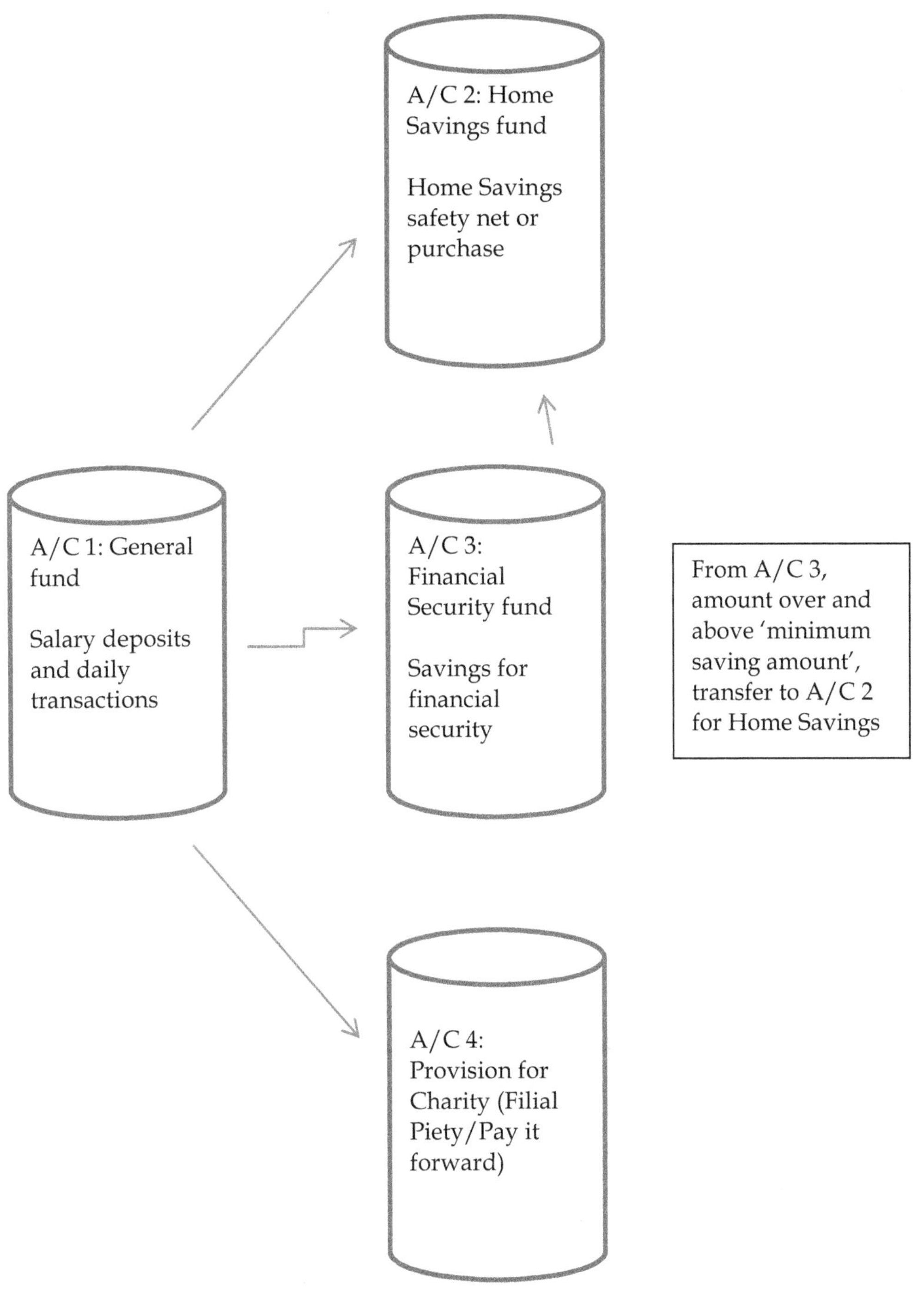

A/C 2: Home Savings fund

Home Savings safety net or purchase

A/C 1: General fund

Salary deposits and daily transactions

A/C 3: Financial Security fund

Savings for financial security

From A/C 3, amount over and above 'minimum saving amount', transfer to A/C 2 for Home Savings

A/C 4: Provision for Charity (Filial Piety/Pay it forward)

Provident Fund

If you are in employment, it is likely that your company is contributing to your provident fund. Consider this fund as a start and part of your retirement savings, namely Financial Security fund (Account Category 3).

If you are self-employed in the 'Gig economy', you will not receive any monthly contribution to your provident fund. In Singapore, for an employee up to 55 years of age, the current rate of employer contribution to the Central Provident Fund is 17% of salaries and 20% is deducted from employees' salaries.[21] So being in employment has its benefits, something to consider when deciding between employment and freelancing.

With 37% of salary accumulating in an employee's provident fund account, it would be wise to research and understand how one's fund is organised, how it grows and how the fund can be used for one's financial requirements.

---

[21] Central Provident Fund Board, Singapore
https://www.cpf.gov.sg/Employers/EmployerGuides/employer-guides/paying-cpf-contributions/cpf-contribution-and-allocation-rates

Table 6.1: Accounts Organisation

Account Category	Account Type	Purpose	Remarks	First Milestone
Account 1 General fund	Savings	Receive salary and daily transactions	Beginning of each month, transfer as budgeted to Accounts 2, 3 & 4.	Co-payment amount for hospitalization & surgery.[22]
Account 2 Home Savings fund	Fixed Deposit	Savings for home purchase or home savings safety net	Monthly transfers from Account 1 (General fund)	10% of estimated cost of targeted home

---

[22] A SS$3,000 payment cap each year is the minimum requirement set by the Ministry of Health in Singapore for an Integrated Shield Plan + Copay Rider.

Table 6.1: Continued

Account Category	Account Type	Purpose	Remarks	First Milestone
Account 3 Financial Security fund	Fixed Deposit	Savings for Financial Security	Monthly transfers from Account 1 (General fund) Amount over and above 'minimum saving amount', transfer to Account 2 for home savings[23]	12 months' worth of monthly expenses- 'minimum savings amount' (emergency fund)
Account 4 Provision for Charity (Filial Piety/Pay it forward)	Fixed Deposit	Provision for charitable contributions	Monthly transfers (nominal amount) from Account 1 (General fund)	

---

[23] Once funds in Account 3 (Financial security fund) have reached the 'minimum savings amount', any excess amount should be transferred to Account 2 (Home savings fund) to build up enough home savings for a down payment.

Chapter 7

Overview of the Journey

Step 3 of Action Plan: Prepare a Cash Assets Projection

Navigational apps such as Google Maps and Waze help us find the shortest routes possible to our destinations. The apps help drivers find directions and avoid traffic jams in real time. For the selected route, the app displays an overview of the route with the distance to the destination and the estimated time of the journey.

Similarly, a Cash Assets Projection shows an 'overview of a financial journey' and the associated timeline. It also displays various milestones with estimated times to reach each point. These milestones serve as signposts in your journey towards your goals. In other words, it helps answer 'When will' questions, namely:

- When will my savings reach 12 months' worth of expenses?
- When will I have enough funds for a down payment for a home?
- When will I complete my home mortgage payments?
- When will I have enough funds to purchase a home in cash?
- When will I have enough funds to live without active income?

The source of your cash inflow is primarily contributions to your provident fund savings and the budgeted monthly savings which is after factoring in all other expenses including personal income taxes.

Cash inflows to Cash Assets:

- Monthly transfers into your Savings Accounts
- Contributions to your Provident Fund

Cash outflows from Cash Assets:

- Down payment on your Home purchase
- Monthly expenses after you are retired (without active income)

Note: The monthly expenses (including rent or mortgage instalments) during your working life are paid from your income as budgeted. So the inflows and outflows to the Cash Assets are from what is saved into savings (including Central Provident Fund) and what is used from savings, namely for a home purchase and living expenses after retirement.

Cash Assets Projection Example 1 - Starting Salary: S$2,200 per month[24]

Assumptions:

- A working career that starts at the age of 24 years
- Monthly savings of S$400, unchanged until retirement at 63 years old
- Monthly contribution to Central Provident Fund (CPF) as per current (2020) rules[25] (Hence, net pay cheque = S$1,760)
- Yearly personal income tax payments do not change the monthly savings
- Yearly salary increment of 1.5% (i.e. net after inflation)
- No disruption in employment income
- Additional expenses due to raising a family and personal lifestyle changes assumed to be covered by increment in income from career advancement and/or income from working spouse
- Purchase of a 3-room public housing flat at age 35 years for S$208,000[26]

Purchase financing:

- Equity portion: S$83,200 (to be paid from CPF ordinary account)
- Mortgage loan: S$124,800 (20 years repayment term, fixed interest rate of 2% per annum)

---

[24] ITE Graduate Employment Survey, Institute of Technical Education, Singapore (2018)
https://www.ite.edu.sg/admissions/graduate-employment-survey
[25] CPF Contribution and Allocation Rates, Central Provident Fund Board, Singapore (2020) https://www.cpf.gov.sg/Employers/EmployerGuides/employer-guides/paying-cpf-contributions/cpf-contribution-and-allocation-rates#Item587
[26] Housing and Development Board, Singapore (2019)
(https://esales.hdb.gov.sg/bp25/launch/19nov/bto/19NOVBTO_page_7523/about0.html

- Instalment: S$632 per month (to be paid from CPF ordinary account)
    - Interior and furniture cost of S$56,000 (to be paid from 'home savings')
- Living expenses upon retirement at 63 years of age assumed to be S$2,540, calculated from a current base of S$1,379 with 1.4% annual inflation rate[27]
- Interest rate assumptions:
    - Compounded annually
    - Savings fixed deposit interest rate: 1.0% per annum
    - CPF interest rates: Ordinary account: 2.5%, Special account: 4%, Medisave account: 4%, Retirement account: 4% (interest rates are per annum)

Minimum Savings Amount is estimated to be S$16,320 based on 1st year monthly expenses of S$1,360 (S$1,760 net pay cheque minus S$400 savings).

Minimum Retirement Amount is estimated to be S$670,560 based on:

- Retirement age of 63 years
- Life Expectancy of 85 years[28], hence 22 years without active income
- Monthly retirement living expenses of S$2,540

---

[27] H.Plecher, "Singapore: Inflation rate from 1984 to 2024" (Statista, Nov. 25, 2019) https://www.statista.com/statistics/379423/inflation-rate-in-singapore/

[28] Public Data, Word Development Bank (April 8, 2020) https://www.google.com/publicdata/explore?ds=d5bncppjof8f9_&met_y=sp_dyn_l e00_in&idim=country:SGP:GBR:HKG&hl=en&dl=en

Table 7.1: Cash Assets Projection Example 1 (S$)[29]

Age	Savings Account	CPF Accounts	Total Savings	Milestone
28	19,173	42,458	61,631	Minimum Savings Amount
35	55,354	136,980	192,335	Home purchase
55	106,108	312,857	418,965	Full homeownership
62	148,561	362,130	510,690	Minimum Retirement Amount
63	154,870	519,275	674,146	Start of Retirement
75	106,499	447,589	554,088	
85	117,641	296,595	414,236	
95	129,949	63,190	193,139	

Cash Assets Projection Example 2: Starting Salary: S$3,000[30]

Assumptions:

- A working career that starts at the age of 24 years
- Monthly savings of S$800, unchanged until retirement at 63 years old
- Monthly contribution to Central Provident Fund (CPF) as per current (2020) rules[31] (Hence, net pay cheque = S$2,400)
- Yearly personal income tax payments do not change the monthly savings
- Yearly salary increment of 1.5% (i.e. net after inflation)
- No disruption in employment income

---

[29] Based on author's financial modeling

[30] Graduate Employment Survey, Ministry of Education, Singapore (2019) https://www.moe.gov.sg/docs/default-source/document/education/post-secondary/files/joint-web-publication-ges-2019.pdf

[31] CPF Contribution and Allocation Rates, Central Provident Fund Board, Singapore (2020) https://www.cpf.gov.sg/Employers/EmployerGuides/employer-guides/paying-cpf-contributions/cpf-contribution-and-allocation-rates#Item587

- Additional expenses due to raising a family and personal lifestyle changes assumed to be covered by increment in income from career advancement and/or income from working spouse
- Purchase of a 3-room public housing flat at age 35 years for S$281,000[32]

Purchase financing:

- Equity portion: S$112,400 (to be paid from CPF Ordinary account)
- Mortgage loan: S$168,600 (20 years repayment term, fixed interest rate of 2%)
- Instalment: S$853 per month (to be paid from CPF Ordinary account)
- Interior and furniture cost of S$70,000 (to be paid from savings)

- Living expenses upon retirement at 63 years of age assumed to be S$2,540, calculated from a current base of S$1,379 with 1.4% annual inflation rate[33]
- Interest rate assumptions:
    - Compounded annually
    - Savings fixed deposit interest rate: 1.0% per annum
    - CPF interest rates: Ordinary account: 2.5%, Special account: 4%, Medisave account: 4%, Retirement account: 4% (interest rates are per annum)

Minimum Savings Amount is estimated to be S$19,200 based on 1st year monthly expenses of S$1,600 per month (S$2,400 net pay cheque minus S$800 savings).

---

[32] Housing and Development Board, Singapore (2019)
https://esales.hdb.gov.sg/bp25/launch/19nov/bto/19NOVBTO_page_7523/about0.html

[33] H.Plecher, "Singapore: Inflation rate from 1984 to 2024", (Statista, Nov. 25, 2019)
https://www.statista.com/statistics/379423/inflation-rate-in-singapore/

Minimum Retirement Amount is estimated to be S$670,560 based on:

- Retirement age of 63 years
- Life Expectancy of 85 years[34], hence 22 years without active income
- Monthly retirement living expenses of S$2,540

Table 7.2: Cash Assets Projection Example 2 (S$)[35]

Age	Savings Account	CPF Accounts	Total Savings	Milestone
27	28,414	42,450	70,864	Minimum Savings Amount
35	110,709	186,791	297,500	Home purchase
55	262,957	430,737	693,694	Full homeownership
55	262,957	430,737	693,694	Minimum Retirement Amount
63	364,685	713,733	1,078,418	Start of Retirement
75	342,924	772,760	1,115,684	
85	378,801	743,529	1,122,330	
95	418,432	734,659	1,153,091	

---

[34] Public Data, Word Development Bank (April 8, 2020)
https://www.google.com/publicdata/explore?ds=d5bncppjof8f9_&met_y=sp_dyn_l
e00_in&idim=country:SGP:GBR:HKG&hl=en&dl=en
[35] Based on author's financial modeling

Step 4 of Action Plan: Set specific objectives to attain your goals and identify interim milestones

Interim milestones can be markers at various points along the journey. Set periodic markers to the following milestones:

- Minimum Savings Amount
- Home Savings - down payment
- Last mortgage payment ('base camp')
- Minimum Retirement Savings ('first peak')

Step 5 of the Action Plan: Monitor your progress

Actual versus Projected Budget

I started my career with an apprenticeship at a manufacturing company in Japan. The assembly line which had fifteen component stations operated by workers had a target of 800 finished (assembled) pieces per 8 hour-shift. After every hour, the person at the last station would count and announce the total finished pieces produced. The objective was to produce 100 component pieces per hour at each station in order to achieve the day's target of 800 finished pieces. The purpose of monitoring every hour was so that the workers could adjust their pace if the hourly target fell short. For example, if they produced 98 pieces in the first hour, they would need to produce 102 pieces in the next hour to catch up to maintain the average pace of 100 pieces per hour. This system of monitoring ensured that the production line met their daily target of 800 pieces. If they did not check and adjust their pace of work every hour, at the end of 8 hours, it would be too late to change the outcome.

Similarly, in order to meet your yearly target according to your cash flow projection, you should monitor your progress every month by comparing your actual expenses with your budget. If you happen to spend more on entertainment this month, then perhaps you need to cut down next month so as to stay within your average for the year.

Actual versus Projected Cash Assets

At the end of each year, check and compare the total of cash balances in your various accounts to the projection to see any significant deviation. Use the new balances to update the cash assets projection. If there is a change in the trajectory of your cash assets projection that may affect your time to reach various milestones, then consider what countermeasures you can take to either increase the inflow or decrease the outflow of cash or both.

Net Worth Dashboard

Calculate the difference in your Net Worth at the beginning and end of each year to check whether your wealth 'increased' or 'deceased' for the year.

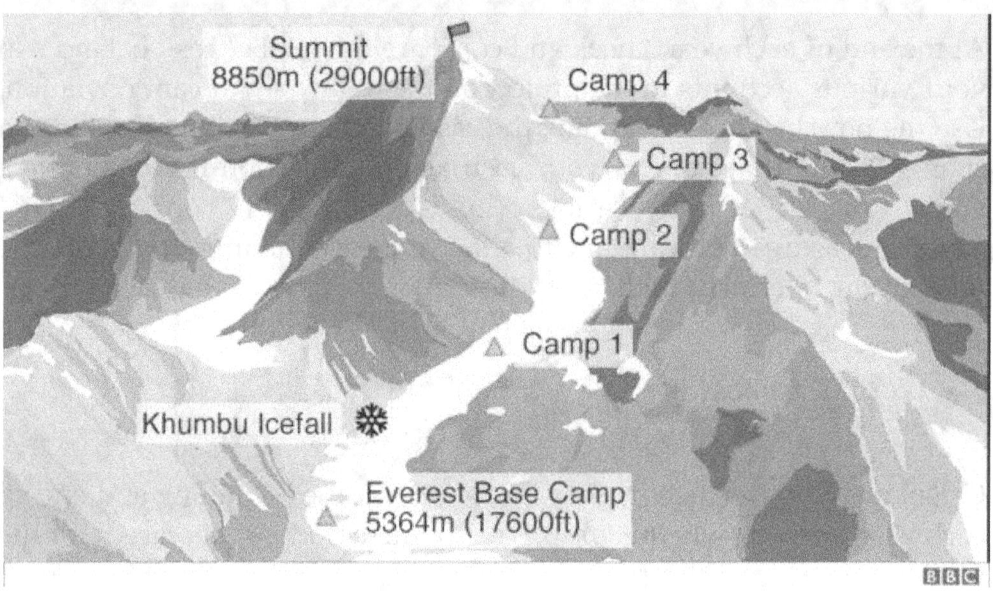

Figure 7.1: "Overview of the Journey to Mount Everest" by Pradeep Bashyal, The Southeast Ridge Route, BBC Nepali (June 8 2019)
https://www.bbc.com/news/world-asia-48464030

Chapter 8

Credit Cards and the Credit Scorekeepers, a Moral Hazard

If you truly believe in the common sense of living within your means, you would probably shape your lifestyle to fit your income. If you do so, you can very likely afford to pay for your monthly expenses according to your budget. This means that you do not need to borrow to meet your monthly expenses. The only exception would be the purchase of a home (property) which can be fulfilled by a mortgage loan.

With the trend towards a cashless society, almost all of us obtain some form of a 'plastic card' to make payments. If you live within your means, then logically a *debit card* could serve the cashless payment function by deducting from your bank account immediately during a transaction. An alternative mode of payment would be 'electronic wallets' (e-wallets) which are online prepaid accounts used to store money.

If you do not need to borrow and can use a debit card or an e-wallet to make cashless payments, then why would you need a *credit card*? The words debit and credit have two very different meanings and yet most people refer to debit cards as credit cards, which wrongly give the impression that you need a credit card to conduct online payments.

If you prefer to have a consolidated bill to pay once a month, in other words, to be 'charged' for the transactions and make a lump sum payment, then a *charge card* serves this purpose. Examples of charge cards are American Express and Diners Club.

Credit card companies such as MasterCard and Visa mainly profit from high interest on credit to customers and commissions from merchants which are factored into the prices of goods. Hence, credit card companies are essentially big moneylenders structured as corporations. Due to their immense marketing prowess, Visa and MasterCard credit cards are now ubiquitous and many establishments only accept these cards as payment modes and not even debit cards issued by the same companies.

From a marketing perspective, a credit card customer has more business value than a debit card customer, measured by the potential to earn interest from credit extension. Hence the relationship with a credit card company is that of a borrower and a moneylender. The interest rates are exorbitant and penalties for default are harsh.

Logically, if you live within your means, then you do not need a credit card. To satisfy establishments that require 'plastic cards', MasterCard and Visa also issue debit cards. By the way, note that all credit cards are issued through commercial banks.

Credit Score

One of the main criteria that a commercial bank considers for a mortgage loan is a potential borrower's credit score (credit rating). A credit score is an indicator of your trustworthiness to repay your debts. Credit card payment records are a component of the credit score. Timely payment of credit card bills reflects on one's financial discipline and hence the chances of obtaining a mortgage loan.

So apparently the situation is such that the banks cannot provide a mortgage loan unless you regularly use a credit card which implies that a person with a credit card debt may have a higher chance of getting a mortgage loan approval than a person without a credit card. I think this situation is absurd. I call it a moral hazard because the 'gatekeepers' of the credit score, the banks, are the same institutions that issue the credit cards, hence making credit card usage a precondition for obtaining loans, a condition that is self-serving to their business.

However, there is another way that a bank can assess your trustworthiness to 'pay your bills on time'- if you deposit a fixed amount every month into a fixed savings account. Although such a scheme does not produce a credit score, it would reflect on your financial discipline and hence factor positively in a loan approval process.

If you want a credit score without a credit card, then the only alternative would be to use a charge card, namely American Express or Diners Club. These charge cards do not have credit lines - monthly bills must be settled in full.

If you prefer having a credit card to generate a credit score, then ensure to pay the monthly bills in full. If you resort to paying the 'minimum amount', you are living beyond your means and reducing your net worth due to high interest rates charged by credit card companies. Also note that if you miss a payment, it will negatively impact your credit score.

Personal Loan

A personal loan often comes with an interest rate so high that it is more than some credit card rates. So stay away from personal loans as well.

Compound Interest on a Loan

Compound interest is the addition of interest to the principal sum of a loan, or in other words, interest on interest. So the law of compounding interest applies to loans as well. Your debts can grow exponentially if you are not able to pay down your loans.

The Rule of 72 also shows how fast a debt can double. With interest rates on credit card debts as high as 25%, inability to pay down or using new debt to pay old debt will lead to doubling of debt in less than 3 years, as calculated by the rule of 72.

These mathematical rules, often applied for investment analysis, also apply to the flip side, which is to unserviceable debts that grow and duplicate. If you end up borrowing to pay interest, you will most likely fall into a debt spiral which is impossible to climb out from without defaulting on your loan which then potentially leads to bankruptcy. The consequences of bankruptcy are very disruptive to one's livelihood, not to mention very stressful.

The average long run return of most businesses is about 10%. So even if your investments provide good returns, there is no logic to justify using loans at exorbitant rates for personal consumption. Spending beyond your means reduces your own financial net worth. Hence, live within your means and avoid borrowing for personal consumption.

Predatory Lending

"By definition, predatory lending benefits the lender and ignores or hinders the borrower's ability to repay the debt. These lending tactics often try to take advantage of a borrower's lack of understanding about loans, terms or finances."[36] The definition also covers any practice that convinces a borrower to accept unfair terms by deceptive means for a loan that a borrower does not need or does not want. For example, a predatory lender may insert credit insurance on auto loans or try to add high service fees for a mortgage loan. Such practices are considered predatory if they are made conditional to the loan on a "take it or leave it" basis.[37]

Comparing the 10% historical average return of most businesses[38] to the 25% average return from consumer lending[39], it is no surprise why many big businesses want to get into the money lending game. Retail giants tend to form affiliated companies to provide financing to purchase their consumer products.

---

[36] Bill Fay, "Predatory Lending: Laws & Unfair Practices" (Debt.org, 2020) https://www.debt.org/credit/predatory-lending/

[37] Brian O'Connell, "What is Predatory Lending" (TheStreet, May 9, 2019) https://www.thestreet.com/personal-finance/mortgages/what-is-predatory-lending-14953861

[38] James Royal, Ph.D. & Arielle O'Shea, "What is the Average Stock Market Return" (nerdwallet, April 2, 2020) https://www.nerdwallet.com/blog/investing/average-stock-market-return/

[39] Duckju Kang, "Average Interest Rates of Credit Cards" (ValueChampion, 2019) https://www.valuechampion.sg/average-interest-rate-credit-cards

Even ride-hailing company Grab with a ready customer base of drivers had started money lending in the guise of 'advance payment' with a deduction for an 'administrative fee' which was essentially an interest charge.[40] The company has now applied for a digital banking license in Singapore.[41] Gaming company Razer, another company that has applied for a digital banking license in Singapore, has a ready customer base of young 'gamers' to whom the company will likely target their lending.[42]

Programs driven by algorithms based on artificial intelligence already entice consumers through continuous messages promoting loans packaged in various forms to the gullible public. This trend will only escalate to the detriment of household financial wellbeing. Be wary of marketing ploys, maintain an appropriate level of scepticism and stay away from temptations that will put you in debt.

[40] Jonathan Chang, Commentary: "Isn't Grab's cash advance scheme a loan programme?" (CNA International Edition, Nov. 28, 2019) https://www.channelnewsasia.com/news/commentary/grab-upfront-cash-advance-program-loan-debt-regulation-law-12130362

[41] Saheli Roy Choudhury, "Grab says it will apply for digital bank license with Singtel" (CNBC, Dec. 29, 2019) https://www.cnbc.com/2019/12/30/grab-says-to-apply-for-singapore-digital-bank-license-with-singtel.html

[42] Aw Cheng Wei, "Gaming company Razer applies to be digital full bank" (The Straits Times, Jan. 2, 2020) https://www.straitstimes.com/business/banking/gaming-company-razer-applies-to-be-a-digital-full-bank

Debt Bondage

Figure 8.1: "Man being imprisoned by credit card debts" by Thongchai
Piwanna (123RF) https://www.123rf.com

Chapter 9

Employment or Entrepreneurship?

Using Mount Everest as an analogy again, there are two main routes for the climb, the Southeast and the Northeast routes. The Southeast is the most frequented route because it is generally considered safer and more accessible.[43]

Similarly, employment and entrepreneurship are two main routes to financial independence. A career as an employee with a lifetime of progression is a relatively stable and predictable path towards financial independence. Entrepreneurship can be a faster route to the 'peaks' but an unexpected 'fall' can also be very devastating with the many twists and turns of running a business. Which route you take depends on your own preference, individual ability, and attitude towards work, personal circumstances and opportunities that arise in your working life. Should you choose to become an entrepreneur, structure your business such that you 'ring fence' your core personal assets, especially your home. Businesses need capital to grow. There are two types of capital, equity and debt. Debt financing for private businesses always requires a personal guarantee from the owner(s). Providing a personal guarantee means that if the company is unable to repay its debt, then the guarantor is personally responsible. Know when to cut your losses as a business owner. Remember that you need a 'roof over your head' even if your business fails. Hence, consider other equity sources for funding your capital requirements and only consider debt financing as a last resort and that too within limits. Seek advice from a trusted advisor on business finance matters but always make decisions objectively.

---

[43] Topchinatravel.com (2004) https://www.topchinatravel.com/mount-everest/climbing-routes-on-mount-everest.htm

Strategise

Keep thinking of how to ensure a continuous stream of income. If you are an employee, ask yourself how to always have a job until retirement. In other words, how can I remain employable? In today's rapidly changing business environment, in order to remain relevant, continuous learning is necessary to enhance personal development, competitiveness and, hence, employability.

If you are an entrepreneur, ask yourself how to achieve sustainable profits for your business or businesses. Exploitation of new ideas is crucial to a business being able to improve its processes, bring new and improved products and services to the market and increase its efficiency, all of which are drivers of profitability. This is essentially the definition of innovation; hence the need to always think 'outside the box'.

Chapter 10

Covid-19 Pandemic

Sometimes we come across news articles or watch video documentaries about how a person living 'pay cheque to pay cheque' or 'hand to mouth' is 'one emergency away from becoming homeless'. We may feel momentarily sympathetic but because it is someone else's predicament, we tend not to give it a second thought.

The Covid-19 pandemic brought global economic activity to a standstill and hence no one was immune to the impact of this crisis. In fact, it brought many financially vulnerable people nearer to the state of being 'one emergency away from becoming homeless'. Many others had to dip into their savings to cover living expenses. The only thing that slowed and prevented the slide into dire straits is governments' interventions in various forms ranging from cash hand-outs to debt moratoriums to help tide their citizens over this period. Even with government support measures for businesses, many jobs have been lost which has affected peoples' ability to pay rent or home mortgage instalments. Governments' financial support can only sustain us temporarily during the mandatory stay-home period after which we will have to be self-reliant again. For those people whose income streams were disrupted and did not resume even after the reopening of the economy, having adequate emergency savings would be especially crucial for their livelihoods.

A survey conducted by OCBC Bank during the lockdown period found that around two-thirds of working Singaporeans and permanent residents had indicated that they did not have enough savings to last them beyond six months, hence the case to drive home the message of the necessity of a 'minimum savings amount' (emergency fund).[44]

The economic impact of the Covid-19 pandemic is a stark reminder to many of us on the basic survival needs, namely shelter, food, medicines and income to pay for these needs. So ensuring the security of our basic needs must be fundamental to our personal financial planning of which 'shelter' is the biggest cost component. Hence owning your home or having adequate home savings is not an option and you should have a plan to achieve this goal.

<hr>

[44] Aw Cheng Wei, "2 in 3 working Singaporeans do not have savings to last them beyond 6 months: OCBC survey" (The Straits Times, June 1, 2020)
https://www.straitstimes.com/business/banking/2-in-3-working-singaporeans-do-not-have-savings-to-last-them-beyond-6-months-ocbc

Chapter 11

Physical Health Dashboard

"Health is Wealth"- Ralph Waldo Emerson

Simply put, to generate income, you have to work and you cannot work productively if you are ill. During the Covid-19 pandemic, the preventive measures adopted worldwide and their impacts on the global economy are testament to the fact that without good health, you cannot engage in economic activities that create wealth.

I am not a physician but this handbook was written in the spirit of a parent's concern for his children's well-being of which health is an integral part. So below are some common health tips that will go a long way in promoting a healthy life. Although some of the chronic diseases may not be of concern until you turn 40 years of age, developing healthy habits early on is part of preventive care. Hence it is important to have a basic understanding of the common chronic diseases in order to appreciate the need to be proactive while you are still young adults. Be proactive to understand and manage common chronic diseases, namely *high blood pressure, high blood cholesterol and diabetes.*[45]

---

[45] Ministry of Health, Singapore https://www.healthhub.sg/a-z/diseases-and-conditions/96/topics_chronic_diseases

High Blood Pressure

High blood pressure refers to the condition in which the blood is pumped around the body at too high a pressure.[46]

Table 11.1: Blood pressure guidelines

Blood pressure	Systolic BP (mmHg)	Diastolic BP (mmHg)
Normal	Less than 130	Less than 80
Borderline	130-139	80-89
High	140-159	90-99
Very High	160 or greater	100 or greater

High Blood Cholesterol

Cholesterol is used by the body for producing hormones, protecting nerves, building cells and other important functions.[47]

Types of Cholesterol

- Low Density Lipoprotein (LDL) is bad cholesterol because too much LDL in your blood can cause your arteries to become narrow and hard (atherosclerosis).
- High Density Lipoprotein (HDL) is good cholesterol because it prevents excess cholesterol from building up in the blood vessel.

---

[46] Ministry of Health, Singapore https://www.healthhub.sg/a-z/diseases-and-conditions/53/highbloodpressure

[47] Ministry of Health, Singapore https://www.healthhub.sg/a-z/diseases-and-conditions/52/highbloodcholesterol

- Triglycerides are a form of fat from food in your blood that is used by your muscles as energy. High levels can increase your risk of heart disease.

Table 11.2: Cholesterol level guidelines

Test	Desirable levels (mmol/L)
Total cholesterol	<5.2
HDL – cholesterol	1.0 - 1.5
LDL – cholesterol	< 3.4
Triglycerides	< 2.3

If your total and LDL cholesterol levels get too high and HDL cholesterol too low, you will be at an increased risk of getting your arteries choked from deposits of cholesterol. If left unchecked, the narrowing of the arteries over time will reduce blood flow. This can lead to conditions such as heart attack or stroke.

Diabetes

Diabetes is a medical condition in which the blood glucose levels remain persistently higher than normal.[48] Our body breaks down some of the food we eat into sugars including glucose and releases it into the blood. To help the sugar enter our cells and provide us with energy, the pancreas produces a hormone called insulin. When there is a lack of insulin, this results in the sugar remaining in the bloodstream.

---

[48] Ministry of Health, Singapore https://www.healthhub.sg/a-z/diseases-and-conditions/102/topics_diabetes

Type 2 diabetes is the most common form of diabetes, usually found in adults. It is when the body does not use insulin properly or does not produce enough of it.

Type 1 diabetes is usually found in children and young adults, where the body produces little or no insulin.

Risk factors for Type 2 diabetes

- Age (especially if you are 40 years old and above)
- Family history of diabetes
- Medical conditions such as high blood pressure, high blood cholesterol or pre-diabetes[49]
- Unhealthy diet
- Overweight (BMI of 23kg/m2 or above)
- Sedentary lifestyle

The Medical Triad

High blood pressure, high blood cholesterol and diabetes are diseases that are linked and people with one of the three diseases are at higher risk of developing one or both of the other diseases.[50] Hence, it is important to be aware and to take preventive measures early on in our lives.

---

[49] Prediabetes is when your blood sugar level is higher than normal but not high enough to be considered diabetic. People with type 2 diabetes almost always had prediabetes first.
Ministry of Health, Singapore https://www.healthhub.sg/a-z/diseases-and-conditions/730/Understanding-Prediabetes-Signs-Symptoms-and-Treatment
[50] Lana Barhum, Reviewed by Maria S. Prelipcean, MD "The link between diabetes and hypertension" (MEDICALNEWSTODAY, May 28, 2019) https://www.medicalnewstoday.com/articles/317220

Healthy Lifestyle

Healthy lifestyle = Balanced diet + Exercise + Stress Management

Table 11.3: Balanced Diet Meal[51]

Percentage	Nutrients
25%	Whole-grain carbohydrates
25%	Proteins
50%	Vegetables & fruits

Maintain Weight

To reduce risk of health problems, try to achieve a healthy body weight and maintain calorie balance.

Energy IN = Energy OUT => Weight maintained

Energy IN > Energy OUT => Weight gain => Health problems

Energy IN < Energy OUT => Weight loss => Health problems[52]

---

[51] Ministry of Health, Singapore
https://www.healthhub.sg/live-healthy/1834/makan-matters-whats-a-healthy-diet
[52] Unless a person was overweight or obese to begin with, weight loss can lead to health problems.

Body Mass Index (BMI)

BMI measures the relationship between weight and height. It is highly correlated with body fat in adults and helps determine whether you are at risk for weight-related health problems.

BMI = Weight (kg) / Height (metres) x Height (metres)

Table 11.4: BMI guidelines in Singapore[53,54]

BMI (kg/sqm)	Category	Risk
Below 18.5	Underweight	Nutritional deficiency
18.5 - 22.9	Normal weight	Healthy range
23.0 - 27.4	Overweight	Moderate risk
27.5 and above	Obese	High risk

Try to target at least 150 minutes of moderate-intensity aerobic physical activity during the week.

---

[53] Ministry of Health, Singapore
https://www.healthhub.sg/programmes/93/bmi-calculator
[54] "There is scientific evidence that suggests that Asian populations have different associations between BMI, percentage of body fat, and health risks than do European populations." - Dr. Chizuru Nishida, Department of Nutrition for Health and Development, World Health Organization (2004)
https://www.who.int/nutrition/publications/bmi_asia_strategies.pdf

Table 11.5: Activity guidelines[55]

Type	At work / home	While commuting	Exercise
Lifestyle	<ul><li>Household chores</li><li>Taking the stairs</li></ul>	<ul><li>Walk to bus stop</li><li>Strolling / Standing</li></ul>	<ul><li>Physical sports</li></ul>
Aerobic	<ul><li>Manual work</li><li>Mopping</li></ul>	<ul><li>15 minutes brisk walk</li><li>Carrying groceries</li><li>Taking the stairs</li></ul>	<ul><li>Brisk walking</li><li>Jogging</li><li>Sports</li></ul>
Strength	<ul><li>Lifting and moving moderately heavy objects</li></ul>	<ul><li>Carrying groceries</li><li>Taking the stairs</li></ul>	<ul><li>Weight training</li></ul>

[55] Ministry of Health, Singapore
https://www.healthhub.sg/sites/assets/Assets/PDFs/HPB/PhysicalActivityPDFs/NPAG_Summary_Guide.pdf

Stress Management[56]

Stress is a part of modern living. It is unavoidable. Anything that causes a change in your life causes stress. Stress serves a purpose when it provides us with the motivation to scale new challenges or overcome difficulties. Stress only becomes harmful when it is not proportionate to the severity of the situation. Manage your stress and become more productive. Some examples of effective coping strategies are:

- Engage in activities you enjoy
- Practice relaxation techniques
- Talk to someone you trust
- Engage in physical exercises
- Prioritize tasks accordingly
- Love oneself

Happiness Hormones

After a session of vigorous physical exercise, you probably felt a sense of satisfaction and even joyful anticipation of the next workout. You may even have felt a growing confidence in your capabilities. "Responsible for this are biochemical processes and the release of so-called happiness hormones. The most popular ones are endorphins, dopamine and serotonin." Dopamine release makes you more alert, more focused and it improves your concentration. Serotonin is involved in the regulation of the sleep-wake cycle and body temperature, it controls appetite and it lowers pain sensitivity.[57] "Endorphins, which are structurally similar to the drug morphine, are considered natural painkillers because they activate opioid receptors in the brain that help

---

[56] "Overcoming Stress", Institute of Mental Health, Singapore (2012)
https://www.imh.com.sg/wellness/page.aspx?id=356
[57] Seana, "Happiness hormones: how training makes you happy" (Well-being, 2014)
https://www.freeletics.com/en/blog/posts/happiness-hormones-training-makes-happy/

minimize discomfort", as explained by J. Kip Matthews, PhD, a sport and exercise psychologist.[58] These hormones can also help bring about feelings of euphoria and general well-being. Hence, regular exercise leads to a sustainable improvement of concentration and an increase of happiness and satisfaction. It is amazing that our bodies have the internal resources to make us feel happy.

[58] Kristen Domonell, "Why endorphins (and exercise) make you happy" (CNN health, Jan. 23, 2016) https://edition.cnn.com/2016/01/13/health/endorphins-exercise-cause-happiness/index.html

Chapter 12

Life Tips

Purpose versus Passion

What drives us to work every day is the need for income, in other words the primary purpose of work is to earn money. Having this sense of purpose is what motivates us to work and being passionate about our work helps uplift our spirits, and consequently enables us to be more productive. Similarly, setting goals gives us a sense of purpose that motivates us to work towards accomplishing them.

Motivation

A lot has been said and written about how important it is to set goals, have an action plan, set measurable objectives, etcetera. Consider also asking yourself *'how not to end up in an undesirable situation'*. It can be an effective motivator.

Problem Solving

"Focus on the solution, not on the problem."- *Jim Rohn*

Let me illustrate the above mentioned quote with 'The Bata shoes story'.

"At the end of the nineteenth century, just as colonial Africa was opening up as a market; all the manufacturers of shoes in Victorian England sent their representatives to Africa to see if there might be an opportunity there for their wares. All duly came back in time with the same answer. 'Nobody in Africa wears shoes. So, there is no market for our products there.' All, that is, save for the Bata representative. He came back saying, 'Nobody in Africa wears shoes. So, there's a huge market for our products in Africa!'"[59]

Decision-making

Seek advice when faced with situations never encountered before. Getting opinions is part of the 'optimal decision making process'. However, think objectively; when considering facts, do not be influenced by personal feelings or opinions. Always make informed decisions - research, and listen to different viewpoints. On a more personal note, share your thoughts with someone you are close to - you may receive emotional support, new knowledge and perhaps even unexpectedly useful insight.

Take Care of Yourself

"If you are travelling with a child or someone who requires assistance, secure your oxygen mask on first, and then assist the other person."[60]*- Excerpt from an inflight passenger announcement script.*

---

[59] Ken Burnett, Opinion article (kenburnett.com, 2011)
http://www.kenburnett.com/BlogTheBataShoesStory.html
[60] Sergio Ortega, (airodyssey.net,1998) https://airodyssey.net/reference/inflight/

In an airline emergency, by attending to your own oxygen needs first, it ensures you will have the mental and physical abilities needed to take care of someone who requires assistance. Analogously in life, taking care of yourself before attending to others is not to be considered as selfish. You can only help others if you have both the mental and physical capacities to do so and both require adequate financial capacity.

Personal Development

From a parent's perspective, personal development is encouraged to help you realize your full potential. Whether you are in employment or run your own business, you and your business must stay relevant to your work and market environment. Keep track of trends related to your work and continuously acquire new knowledge. Do not be afraid to try new things, it is a matter of 'getting used to them' and science has proved this point. "Neuroplasticity is the brain's ability to reorganise itself by forming new neural connections throughout life."[61] In other words, we have the capability to learn new things throughout our lives.

Marketing Ploys

Be wary of all forms of marketing ploys including predatory lending. Don't be too quick to embrace popular opinion. Keep any relationship with bankers strictly transactional and remember that you are ultimately responsible for your own financial choices. So do not invest in any product you do not understand.

---

[61] William C. Shiel Jr., MD, FACP, FACR, "Medical Definition of Neuroplasticity" (MedicineNet, Jan. 24, 2017)
https://www.medicinenet.com/script/main/art.asp?articlekey=40362

Cautionary Tales

Just before the 2008 financial crisis, investment bankers promoted the bonds of Lehman Brothers, a global financial services firm, despite probably knowing that the company's financial position was on shaky ground. Following the collapse of Lehman Brothers, about 10,000 retail investors in Singapore lost all or a large part of their investments totalling about S$500 million.[62]

In a more recent case involving Hyflux Ltd., a water treatment company, 34,000 retail investors stand to lose all or a large part of their investments in bonds totalling S$900 million. A year before the company filed for bankruptcy, the bonds were promoted to retail investors, many of whom were retirees, despite the investment bankers probably knowing that the company was not in good financial shape.[63]

Healthy Body and Mind

Do not take for granted your good physical condition and sound mental health. Treat your body with reverence as you would a person you revere.

"Count your blessings!"

---

[62] Valerie Chew, "Lehman Brothers Minibond saga" (Singapore Infopedia, March 3, 2010) https://eresources.nlb.gov.sg/infopedia/articles/SIP_1654_2010-03-19.html
[63] Andy Mukherjee, "Don't blame Singapore investors for Hyflux loss" (Bloomberg, April 10, 2019)
https://sg.finance.yahoo.com/news/dont-blame-singapore-investors-hyflux-loss-andy-mukherjee-023106678.html

Conclusion

The desire for financial security of which homeownership and adequate retirement savings are key components, is inherent in all of us regardless of our socioeconomic position in life. While building up a 'minimum retirement savings' is a necessary goal to aspire to, achieving 'full retirement amount' is an ideal depending on your personal aspirations.

Financial goals have underlying purposes. Having peace of mind that you have a roof over your head and enough income or savings to cover your expenses is a state of mind one tends to take for granted. However, financial security is necessary for your mind to focus on other issues in life that also matter to you. It would be especially challenging, if not impossible, to fulfil your financial objectives when you are unable to work for income. Hence, it is important to recognize your financial goals early on so that you have time to plan and work towards achieving them.

You deserve to live life to your fullest potential without the feeling of being insecure.

"Be All You Can Be" - E.N.J. Carter[64]

---

[64] "Be All You Can Be" was the recruiting slogan of the United States Army for over twenty years. Earl Carter (pen-name, E.N.J. Carter) working for the N.W. Ayer Advertising Agency as a Senior Copywriter created the "Be All You Can Be" theme line in 1980.

Acknowledgements

My completion of this project could not have been accomplished without the support of my two sons and my niece. Thank you all for taking the time to read the draft manuscripts and provide valuable feedback.

To my caring, loving and supportive wife, your encouragement and belief in me gives me strength to overcome life's challenges. I am eternally grateful.

About the Author

SK Read was a senior business executive with over thirty years of experience in industrial management encompassing finance, operations, marketing and human resources. He was an adjunct lecturer for fourteen years at various universities teaching management related courses, namely Operations Management, Business Management and Managerial Psychology.

He is now devoting his time and energy to educating the young as he believes his life experience and passion for teaching places him in a unique position to act as a conduit between the business and academic environments. He conducts co-curricular workshops at educational institutions to provide students with essential life skills with a focus on financial literacy and social entrepreneurship.